This book is copyright protected. Please do not reproduce in either electronic means or in printed format except for your explicit personal use. This means that copying this book is prohibited and not allowed without permission from the author.
All Rights Reserved

My Prayer Journal
(Catholic Edition)

- ❖ Daily Reflections
- ❖ Scripture Reading
- ❖ Daily Prayers
- ❖ Intercession Through Mary
- ❖ Praying the Rosary
- ❖ Praise and Thanksgiving
- ❖ Confessions

The Rosary Cheat Sheet

1. Make the Sign of the Cross and say the "Apostles Creed."
2. Say the "Our Father."
3. Say three " Hail Marys."
4. Say the "Glory Be to the Father."
5. Announce the first Mystery and say the "Our Father."
6. Say ten "Hail Marys" while meditating on the Mystery.
7. Say the "Glory Be to the Father" and the "Fatima Prayer."
8. Announce the second Mystery and say the "Our Father. " Repeat steps 6 and 7 and continue the third, fourth and fifth Mysteries in the same manner.
9. Say the "Hail Holy Queen."
10. Say the "Prayer After the Rosary"

The Mysteries Cheat Sheet

- ❖ **The Joyful Mysteries**

1. **The Annunciation (Humility) Luke 1:26-38**
   The Angel Gabriel appears to Mary, announcing she is to be the Mother of God
2. **The Visitation (Charity) Luke 1:39-56**
   Elizabeth greets Mary: "Blessed art Thou amongst women and blessed is the fruit of thy womb!"
3. **The Nativity (Poverty) Luke 2:1-20**
   The Virgin Mary gives birth to the Redeemer of the World.
4. **The Presentation (Obedience) Luke 2:22-39**
   The Blessed Mother presents the Child Jesus in the Temple
5. **Finding in the Temple (Piety) Luke 2:42-52**
   The Blessed Mother finds Jesus in the Temple.

The Mysteries Cheat Sheet

- ❖ **The Luminous Mysteries**

1. **The Baptism of Christ in the Jordan John 1:29-34**
   The heavens open wide and the voice of the Father declares Jesus the beloved Son
2. **The Wedding Feast at Cana John 2:1-11**
   The first of the signs, when Christ changes water into wine and opens the hearts of the disciples to faith, thanks to the intervention of Mary, the first among believers.
3. **The Announcement of the Kingdom Matthew 4:17**
   Jesus proclaims the coming of the Kingdom of God, calls us to conversion and forgives the sins of all who draw near to Him in humble trust.
4. **The Transfiguration Matthew 17:1-8**
   The glory of the Godhead shines forth from the face of Christ as the Father commands the astonished Apostles to "listen to him."
5. **The Institution of the Eucharist (food for our salvation) Matthew 26:26-30**
   Christ offers his body and blood as food under the signs of bread and wine, and testifies "to the end" His love for humanity, for whose salvation He will offer Himself in sacrifice.

The Mysteries Cheat Sheet

❖ **The Sorrowful Mysteries**

1. **The Agony in the Garden (Contrition) Luke 22:39-44**
   At Gethsemane, Jesus prays as He contemplates the sins of the world.
2. **The Scourging at the Pillar (Purity) Matthew 27:26**
   Jesus is cruelly scourged until His mortified body could bear no more.
3. **Crowning with Thorns (Courage) Matthew 27:28-31**
   A crown of thorns is placed on the head of Jesus.
4. **Carrying of the Cross (Patience) Luke 23:26-32**
   Jesus carries the heavy cross upon His shoulders to Calvary.
5. **The Crucifixion (Self-Denial) Matthew 27:33-50**
   Jesus is nailed to the cross and dies after hours of agony.

The Mysteries Cheat Sheet

- ❖ **The Glorious**

1. **The Resurrection (Faith) Matthew 28:1-20**
   Jesus rises glorious and immortal, three days after His death.
2. **The Ascension (Hope) Luke 24:50-51**
   Jesus ascends into Heaven forty days after His Resurrection.
3. **Descent of the Holy Spirit (Love) Acts 2:24**
   The Holy Spirit descends upon Mary and the Apostles.
4. **The Assumption (Eternal Happiness)**
   The Blessed Mother is united with her Divine Son in Heaven.
5. **The Coronation (Devotion to Mary)**
   Mary is gloriously crowned Queen of Heaven and earth.

❖ **Sign Of The Cross**

In the name of the Father, and of the Son, and of the Holy Spirit. Amen.

❖ **The Apostles Creed**

I believe in God, the Father Almighty, Creator of Heaven and earth; and in Jesus Christ, his only Son, our Lord; who was conceived by the Holy Spirit. born of the Virgin Mary, He suffered under Pontius Pilate, was crucified, died and was buried. He descended into hell; the third day He rose again from the dead; he ascended into Heaven sits at the right hand of God, the Father almighty; from there he will come to judge the living and the dead. I believe in the Holy Spirit, the Holy Catholic Church, the Communion of Saints, the forgiveness of sins, the resurrection of the body, and life everlasting, Amen.

❖ **Our Father**

Our Father, who art in Heaven; hallowed by Thy name; Thy kingdom come; Thy will be done on earth as it is in Heaven. Give us this day our daily bread; and forgive us our trespasses as we forgive those who trespass against us, and lead us not into temptation; but deliver us from evil. Amen

❖ Hail Mary

Hail Mary, full of grace, the Lord is with thee. Blessed art thou among women and blessed is the fruit of thy womb, Jesus. Holy Mary, mother of God, pray for us sinners now and at the hour of our death. Amen

❖ Glory Be

Glory be to the Father, to the Son and to the Holy Spirit. As it was in the beginning is now and ever shall be, world without end, Amen. .

❖ Hail, Holy Queen

Hail, Holy Queen, Mother of Mercy, our life, our sweetness and our hope. To thee we cry, poor banished children of Eve. To thee do we send up our sighs, mourning and weeping in this valley of tears. Turn then most gracious advocate, thine eyes of mercy towards us, And after this our exile, show unto us the blessed Fruit of they womb, Jesus. O clement. O loving, O sweet Virgin Mary. Pray for us, O holy Mother of God That we may be made worthy of the promises of Christ.

- ❖ **O My Jesus**

    O my Jesus, forgive us our sins, save us from the fires of hell, and lead all souls to Heaven, especially those in most need of your Mercy. Amen

- ❖ **Prayer After The Rosary:**

    O God, whose only-begotten Son, by His life, death and resurrection, has purchased for us the rewards of eternal life; grant, we beseech Thee, that, meditating upon these mysteries of the Most Holy Rosary of the Blessed Virgin Mary, we may imitate what they contain and obtain what they promise, through the same Christ our Lord. Amen.

    V. May the divine assistance remain always with us.
    R. And may the souls of the faithful departed, through the mercy of God, rest in peace. Amen.

Weekly Prayer Log

"To be a Christian without prayer is no more possible than to be alive without breathing." – Martin Luther

Week: _____

Day	Morning	Evening
Sunday		
Monday		
Tuesday		
Wednesday		
Thursday		
Friday		
Saturday		

Weekly Rosary Mysteries Chart

The Church sets aside Rosary Days to help in praying the Rosary. This is the chart for Ordinary Time

Day	Rosary Mystery	Complete?
Sunday	Glorious Mysteries	
Monday	Joyful Mysteries	
Tuesday	Sorrowful Mysteries	
Wednesday	Glorious Mysteries	
Thursday	Luminous Mysteries	
Friday	Sorrowful Mysteries	
Saturday	Joyful Mysteries	

Daily Prayer

"Prayer is an act of love." -Saint Teresa of Avila

Date:_____

Prayer for Other

Who is God Placing on my Heart?	Scripture References	What God Said

Daily Prayers

"Prayer is an act of love." –Saint Teresa of Avila

Date:_____

Prayer for Myself (Personal Issues and Needs)

What am I praying for?	Scripture References	What God Said

Daily Prayers

"Prayer is an act of love." -Saint Teresa of Avila

Date:_____

Social Issues, World Issues, Governments, Churches

Current political /worldwide issues	Scripture References	What God Said

Intercessions Through Mary

"Most Immaculate heart of Mary, pray for us that we may grow closer to your Son, Jesus."

Date:_____

"Mary, please pray for."

Person or Issue	Specific Prayer Request

Daily Scriptures

"Be Still and Know that I am God." —Psalm 46:10

Date: _____

Scripture Passage: _____

Reflections

- *My heart:*

- *My head:*

- *My hand:*

Answer to Prayers

"Prayer unites us." —Pop Francis

Date: _____

Prayers that God has Answered:

Confessions

"Those who hope in the Lord will review their strength. They will soar on wings like eagles." —Isaiah 40:31

Date:_____

My Confession:

Thoughts on self-improvement:

Praise and Thanksgiving

"The best way to show gratitude to God and people is to accept everything with joy." — Mother Theresa

Date: _____

Today I am grateful for:

I will try to give thanks by:

Weekly Prayer Log

"To be a Christian without prayer is no more possible than to be alive without breathing." – Martin Luther

Week:_____

Day	Morning	Evening
Sunday		
Monday		
Tuesday		
Wednesday		
Thursday		
Friday		
Saturday		

Weekly Rosary Mysteries Chart

The Church sets aside Rosary Days to help in praying the Rosary. This is the chart for Ordinary Time

Day	Rosary Mystery	Complete?
Sunday	Glorious Mysteries	
Monday	Joyful Mysteries	
Tuesday	Sorrowful Mysteries	
Wednesday	Glorious Mysteries	
Thursday	Luminous Mysteries	
Friday	Sorrowful Mysteries	
Saturday	Joyful Mysteries	

Daily Prayer

"Prayer is an act of love." -Saint Teresa of Avila

Date:_____

Prayer for Other

Who is God Placing on my Heart?	Scripture References	What God Said

Daily Prayers

"Prayer is an act of love." -Saint Teresa of Avila

Date:_____

Prayer for Myself (Personal Issues and Needs)

What am I praying for?	Scripture References	What God Said

Daily Prayers

"Prayer is an act of love." -Saint Teresa of Avila

Date:_____

Social Issues, World Issues, Governments, Churches

Current political /worldwide issues	Scripture References	What God Said

Intercessions Through Mary

"Most Immaculate heart of Mary, pray for us that we may grow closer to your Son, Jesus."

Date:_____

"Mary, please pray for."

Person or Issue	Specific Prayer Request

Daily Scriptures

"Be Still and Know that I am God." —Psalm 46:10

Date: _____

Scripture Passage: _____

Reflections

- *My heart:*

- *My head:*

- *My hand:*

Answer to Prayers

"Prayer unites us." — Pop Francis

Date:_____

Prayers that God has Answered:

Confessions

"Those who hope in the Lord will review their strength. They will soar on wings like eagles." —Isaiah 40:31

Date:_____

My Confession:

Thoughts on self-improvement:

Praise and Thanksgiving

"The best way to show gratitude to God and people is to accept everything with joy." —Mother Theresa

Date:_____

Today I am grateful for:

I will try to give thanks by:

Weekly Prayer Log

"To be a Christian without prayer is no more possible than to be alive without breathing." – Martin Luther

Week:_____

Day	Morning	Evening
Sunday		
Monday		
Tuesday		
Wednesday		
Thursday		
Friday		
Saturday		

Weekly Rosary Mysteries Chart

The Church sets aside Rosary Days to help in praying the Rosary. This is the chart for Ordinary Time

Day	Rosary Mystery	Complete?
Sunday	Glorious Mysteries	
Monday	Joyful Mysteries	
Tuesday	Sorrowful Mysteries	
Wednesday	Glorious Mysteries	
Thursday	Luminous Mysteries	
Friday	Sorrowful Mysteries	
Saturday	Joyful Mysteries	

Daily Prayer

"Prayer is an act of love." –Saint Teresa of Avila

Date:_____

Prayer for Other

Who is God Placing on my Heart?	Scripture References	What God Said

Daily Prayers

"Prayer is an act of love." –Saint Teresa of Avila

Date:_____

Prayer for Myself (Personal Issues and Needs)

What am I praying for?	Scripture References	What God Said

Daily Prayers

"Prayer is an act of love." −Saint Teresa of Avila

Date:_____

Social Issues, World Issues, Governments, Churches

Current political /worldwide issues	Scripture References	What God Said

Intercessions Through Mary

"Most Immaculate heart of Mary, pray for us that we may grow closer to your Son, Jesus."

Date:_____

"Mary, please pray for."

Person or Issue	Specific Prayer Request

Daily Scriptures

"Be Still and Know that I am God." —Psalm 46:10

Date: _____

Scripture Passage: _____

Reflections

- My heart:

- My head:

- My hand:

Answer to Prayers

"Prayer unites us." —Pop Francis

Date:_____

Prayers that God has Answered:

Confessions

"Those who hope in the Lord will review their strength. They will soar on wings like eagles." —Isaiah 40:31

Date:_____

My Confession:

Thoughts on self-improvement:

Praise and Thanksgiving

"The best way to show gratitude to God and people is to accept everything with joy." —Mother Theresa

Date:_____

Today I am grateful for:

I will try to give thanks by:

Weekly Prayer Log

"To be a Christian without prayer is no more possible than to be alive without breathing." – Martin Luther

Week: _____

Day	Morning	Evening
Sunday		
Monday		
Tuesday		
Wednesday		
Thursday		
Friday		
Saturday		

Weekly Rosary Mysteries Chart

The Church sets aside Rosary Days to help in praying the Rosary. This is the chart for Ordinary Time

Day	Rosary Mystery	Complete?
Sunday	Glorious Mysteries	
Monday	Joyful Mysteries	
Tuesday	Sorrowful Mysteries	
Wednesday	Glorious Mysteries	
Thursday	Luminous Mysteries	
Friday	Sorrowful Mysteries	
Saturday	Joyful Mysteries	

Daily Prayer

"Prayer is an act of love." -Saint Teresa of Avila

Date:_____

Prayer for Other

Who is God Placing on my Heart?	Scripture References	What God Said

Daily Prayers

"Prayer is an act of love." -Saint Teresa of Avila

Date:_____

Prayer for Myself (Personal Issues and Needs)

What am I praying for?	Scripture References	What God Said

Daily Prayers

"Prayer is an act of love." -Saint Teresa of Avila

Date:_____

Social Issues, World Issues, Governments, Churches

Current political /worldwide issues	Scripture References	What God Said

Intercessions Through Mary

"Most Immaculate heart of Mary, pray for us that we may grow closer to your Son, Jesus."

Date:_____

"Mary, please pray for."

Person or Issue	Specific Prayer Request

Daily Scriptures

"Be Still and Know that I am God." —Psalm 46:10

Date: _____

Scripture Passage: _____

Reflections

- My heart:

- My head:

- My hand:

Answer to Prayers

"Prayer unites us." —Pop Francis

Date: _____

Prayers that God has Answered:

Confessions

"Those who hope in the Lord will review their strength. They will soar on wings like eagles." —Isaiah 40:31

Date:_____

My Confession:

Thoughts on self-improvement:

Praise and Thanksgiving

"The best way to show gratitude to God and people is to accept everything with joy." —Mother Theresa

Date: _____

Today I am grateful for:

I will try to give thanks by:

Weekly Prayer Log

"To be a Christian without prayer is no more possible than to be alive without breathing." - Martin Luther

Week: _____

Day	Morning	Evening
Sunday		
Monday		
Tuesday		
Wednesday		
Thursday		
Friday		
Saturday		

Weekly Rosary Mysteries Chart

The Church sets aside Rosary Days to help in praying the Rosary. This is the chart for Ordinary Time

Day	Rosary Mystery	Complete?
Sunday	Glorious Mysteries	
Monday	Joyful Mysteries	
Tuesday	Sorrowful Mysteries	
Wednesday	Glorious Mysteries	
Thursday	Luminous Mysteries	
Friday	Sorrowful Mysteries	
Saturday	Joyful Mysteries	

Daily Prayer

"Prayer is an act of love." -Saint Teresa of Avila

Date:_____

Prayer for Other

Who is God Placing on my Heart?	Scripture References	What God Said

Daily Prayers

"Prayer is an act of love." -Saint Teresa of Avila

Date:_____

Prayer for Myself (Personal Issues and Needs)

What am I praying for?	Scripture References	What God Said

Daily Prayers

"Prayer is an act of love." -Saint Teresa of Avila

Date:_____

Social Issues, World Issues, Governments, Churches

Current political /worldwide issues	Scripture References	What God Said

Intercessions Through Mary

"Most Immaculate heart of Mary, pray for us that we may grow closer to your Son, Jesus."

Date:_____

"Mary, please pray for."

Person or Issue	Specific Prayer Request

Daily Scriptures

"Be Still and Know that I am God." — Psalm 46:10

Date: _____

Scripture Passage: _____

Reflections

- *My heart:*

- *My head:*

- *My hand:*

Answer to Prayers

"Prayer unites us." —Pop Francis

Date:_____

Prayers that God has Answered:

Confessions

"Those who hope in the Lord will review their strength. They will soar on wings like eagles." —Isaiah 40:31

Date:_____

My Confession:

Thoughts on self-improvement:

Praise and Thanksgiving

"The best way to show gratitude to God and people is to accept everything with joy." —Mother Theresa

Date: _____

Today I am grateful for:

I will try to give thanks by:

Weekly Prayer Log

"To be a Christian without prayer is no more possible than to be alive without breathing." – Martin Luther

Week: _____

Day	Morning	Evening
Sunday		
Monday		
Tuesday		
Wednesday		
Thursday		
Friday		
Saturday		

Weekly Rosary Mysteries Chart

The Church sets aside Rosary Days to help in praying the Rosary. This is the chart for Ordinary Time

Day	Rosary Mystery	Complete?
Sunday	Glorious Mysteries	
Monday	Joyful Mysteries	
Tuesday	Sorrowful Mysteries	
Wednesday	Glorious Mysteries	
Thursday	Luminous Mysteries	
Friday	Sorrowful Mysteries	
Saturday	Joyful Mysteries	

Daily Prayer

"Prayer is an act of love." -Saint Teresa of Avila

Date:_____

Prayer for Other

Who is God Placing on my Heart?	Scripture References	What God Said

Daily Prayers

"Prayer is an act of love." –Saint Teresa of Avila

Date:_____

Prayer for Myself (Personal Issues and Needs)

What am I praying for?	Scripture References	What God Said

Daily Prayers

"Prayer is an act of love." –Saint Teresa of Avila

Date:_____

Social Issues, World Issues, Governments, Churches

Current political /worldwide issues	Scripture References	What God Said

Intercessions Through Mary

"Most Immaculate heart of Mary, pray for us that we may grow closer to your Son, Jesus."

Date:_____

"Mary, please pray for."

Person or Issue	Specific Prayer Request

Daily Scriptures

"Be Still and Know that I am God." —Psalm 46:10

Date: _____

Scripture Passage: _____

Reflections

- *My heart:*

- *My head:*

- *My hand:*

Answer to Prayers

"Prayer unites us." —Pop Francis

Date:_____

Prayers that God has Answered:

Confessions

"Those who hope in the Lord will review their strength. They will soar on wings like eagles." —Isaiah 40:31

Date:_____

My Confession:

Thoughts on self-improvement:

Praise and Thanksgiving

"The best way to show gratitude to God and people is to accept everything with joy." —Mother Theresa

Date:_____

Today I am grateful for:

I will try to give thanks by:

Weekly Prayer Log

"To be a Christian without prayer is no more possible than to be alive without breathing." – Martin Luther

Week: _____

Day	Morning	Evening
Sunday		
Monday		
Tuesday		
Wednesday		
Thursday		
Friday		
Saturday		

Weekly Rosary Mysteries Chart

The Church sets aside Rosary Days to help in praying the Rosary. This is the chart for Ordinary Time

Day	Rosary Mystery	Complete?
Sunday	Glorious Mysteries	
Monday	Joyful Mysteries	
Tuesday	Sorrowful Mysteries	
Wednesday	Glorious Mysteries	
Thursday	Luminous Mysteries	
Friday	Sorrowful Mysteries	
Saturday	Joyful Mysteries	

Daily Prayer

"Prayer is an act of love." – Saint Teresa of Avila

Date:_____

Prayer for Other

Who is God Placing on my Heart?	Scripture References	What God Said

Daily Prayers

"Prayer is an act of love." –Saint Teresa of Avila

Date:_____

Prayer for Myself (Personal Issues and Needs)

What am I praying for?	Scripture References	What God Said

Daily Prayers

"Prayer is an act of love." -Saint Teresa of Avila

Date:_____

Social Issues, World Issues, Governments, Churches

Current political /worldwide issues	Scripture References	What God Said

Intercessions Through Mary

"Most Immaculate heart of Mary, pray for us that we may grow closer to your Son, Jesus."

Date:_____

"Mary, please pray for."

Person or Issue	Specific Prayer Request

Daily Scriptures

"Be Still and Know that I am God." —Psalm 46:10

Date: _____

Scripture Passage: _____

Reflections

- My heart:

- My head:

- My hand:

Answer to Prayers

"Prayer unites us." —Pop Francis

Date:_____

Prayers that God has Answered:

Confessions

"Those who hope in the Lord will review their strength. They will soar on wings like eagles." —Isaiah 40:31

Date:_____

My Confession:

Thoughts on self-improvement:

Praise and Thanksgiving

"The best way to show gratitude to God and people is to accept everything with joy." —Mother Theresa

Date:_____

Today I am grateful for:

I will try to give thanks by:

Weekly Prayer Log

"To be a Christian without prayer is no more possible than to be alive without breathing." – Martin Luther

Week: _____

Day	Morning	Evening
Sunday		
Monday		
Tuesday		
Wednesday		
Thursday		
Friday		
Saturday		

Weekly Rosary Mysteries Chart

The Church sets aside Rosary Days to help in praying the Rosary. This is the chart for Ordinary Time

Day	Rosary Mystery	Complete?
Sunday	Glorious Mysteries	
Monday	Joyful Mysteries	
Tuesday	Sorrowful Mysteries	
Wednesday	Glorious Mysteries	
Thursday	Luminous Mysteries	
Friday	Sorrowful Mysteries	
Saturday	Joyful Mysteries	

Daily Prayer

"Prayer is an act of love." -Saint Teresa of Avila

Date:_____

Prayer for Other

Who is God Placing on my Heart?	Scripture References	What God Said

Daily Prayers

"Prayer is an act of love." –Saint Teresa of Avila

Date:_____

Prayer for Myself (Personal Issues and Needs)

What am I praying for?	Scripture References	What God Said

Daily Prayers

"Prayer is an act of love." -Saint Teresa of Avila

Date:_____

Social Issues, World Issues, Governments, Churches

Current political /worldwide issues	Scripture References	What God Said

Intercessions Through Mary

"Most Immaculate heart of Mary, pray for us that we may grow closer to your Son, Jesus."

Date:_____

"Mary, please pray for."

Person or Issue	Specific Prayer Request

Daily Scriptures

"Be Still and Know that I am God." —Psalm 46:10

Date: _____

Scripture Passage: _____

Reflections

- My heart:

- My head:

- My hand:

Answer to Prayers

"Prayer unites us." —Pop Francis

Date:_____

Prayers that God has Answered:

Confessions

"Those who hope in the Lord will review their strength. They will soar on wings like eagles." —Isaiah 40:31

Date:_____

My Confession:

Thoughts on self-improvement:

Praise and Thanksgiving

"The best way to show gratitude to God and people is to accept everything with joy." —Mother Theresa

Date:_____

Today I am grateful for:

I will try to give thanks by:

Weekly Prayer Log

"To be a Christian without prayer is no more possible than to be alive without breathing." – Martin Luther

Week: _____

Day	Morning	Evening
Sunday		
Monday		
Tuesday		
Wednesday		
Thursday		
Friday		
Saturday		

Weekly Rosary Mysteries Chart

The Church sets aside Rosary Days to help in praying the Rosary. This is the chart for Ordinary Time

Day	Rosary Mystery	Complete?
Sunday	Glorious Mysteries	
Monday	Joyful Mysteries	
Tuesday	Sorrowful Mysteries	
Wednesday	Glorious Mysteries	
Thursday	Luminous Mysteries	
Friday	Sorrowful Mysteries	
Saturday	Joyful Mysteries	

Daily Prayer

"Prayer is an act of love." –Saint Teresa of Avila

Date:_____

Prayer for Other

Who is God Placing on my Heart?	Scripture References	What God Said

Daily Prayers

"Prayer is an act of love." –Saint Teresa of Avila

Date:_____

Prayer for Myself (Personal Issues and Needs)

What am I praying for?	Scripture References	What God Said

Daily Prayers

"Prayer is an act of love." -Saint Teresa of Avila

Date:_____

Social Issues, World Issues, Governments, Churches

Current political /worldwide issues	Scripture References	What God Said

Intercessions Through Mary

"Most Immaculate heart of Mary, pray for us that we may grow closer to your Son, Jesus."

Date:_____

"Mary, please pray for."

Person or Issue	Specific Prayer Request

Daily Scriptures

"Be Still and Know that I am God." —Psalm 46:10

Date: _____

Scripture Passage: _____

Reflections

- *My heart:*

- *My head:*

- *My hand:*

Answer to Prayers

"Prayer unites us." —Pop Francis

Date:_____

Prayers that God has Answered:

Confessions

"Those who hope in the Lord will review their strength. They will soar on wings like eagles." —Isaiah 40:31

Date:_____

My Confession:

Thoughts on self-improvement:

Praise and Thanksgiving

"The best way to show gratitude to God and people is to accept everything with joy." —Mother Theresa

Date:_____

Today I am grateful for:

I will try to give thanks by:

Weekly Prayer Log

"To be a Christian without prayer is no more possible than to be alive without breathing." – Martin Luther

Week: _____

Day	Morning	Evening
Sunday		
Monday		
Tuesday		
Wednesday		
Thursday		
Friday		
Saturday		

Weekly Rosary Mysteries Chart

The Church sets aside Rosary Days to help in praying the Rosary. This is the chart for Ordinary Time

Day	Rosary Mystery	Complete?
Sunday	Glorious Mysteries	
Monday	Joyful Mysteries	
Tuesday	Sorrowful Mysteries	
Wednesday	Glorious Mysteries	
Thursday	Luminous Mysteries	
Friday	Sorrowful Mysteries	
Saturday	Joyful Mysteries	

Daily Prayer

"Prayer is an act of love." –Saint Teresa of Avila

Date:_____

Prayer for Other

Who is God Placing on my Heart?	Scripture References	What God Said

Daily Prayers

"Prayer is an act of love." -Saint Teresa of Avila

Date:_____

Prayer for Myself (Personal Issues and Needs)

What am I praying for?	Scripture References	What God Said

Daily Prayers

"Prayer is an act of love." -Saint Teresa of Avila

Date:_____

Social Issues, World Issues, Governments, Churches

Current political /worldwide issues	Scripture References	What God Said

Intercessions Through Mary

"Most Immaculate heart of Mary, pray for us that we may grow closer to your Son, Jesus."

Date:_____

"Mary, please pray for."

Person or Issue	Specific Prayer Request

Daily Scriptures

"Be Still and Know that I am God." —Psalm 46:10

Date: _____

Scripture Passage: _____

Reflections

- *My heart:*

- *My head:*

- *My hand:*

Answer to Prayers

"Prayer unites us." —Pop Francis

Date:_____

Prayers that God has Answered:

Confessions

"Those who hope in the Lord will review their strength. They will soar on wings like eagles." —Isaiah 40:31

Date: _____

My Confession:

Thoughts on self-improvement:

Praise and Thanksgiving

"The best way to show gratitude to God and people is to accept everything with joy." —Mother Theresa

Date:_____

Today I am grateful for:

I will try to give thanks by:

Weekly Prayer Log

"To be a Christian without prayer is no more possible than to be alive without breathing." – Martin Luther

Week: _____

Day	Morning	Evening
Sunday		
Monday		
Tuesday		
Wednesday		
Thursday		
Friday		
Saturday		

Weekly Rosary Mysteries Chart

The Church sets aside Rosary Days to help in praying the Rosary. This is the chart for Ordinary Time

Day	Rosary Mystery	Complete?
Sunday	Glorious Mysteries	
Monday	Joyful Mysteries	
Tuesday	Sorrowful Mysteries	
Wednesday	Glorious Mysteries	
Thursday	Luminous Mysteries	
Friday	Sorrowful Mysteries	
Saturday	Joyful Mysteries	

Daily Prayer

"Prayer is an act of love." -Saint Teresa of Avila

Date:_____

Prayer for Other

Who is God Placing on my Heart?	Scripture References	What God Said

Daily Prayers

"Prayer is an act of love." -Saint Teresa of Avila

Date:_____

Prayer for Myself (Personal Issues and Needs)

What am I praying for?	Scripture References	What God Said

Daily Prayers

"Prayer is an act of love." -Saint Teresa of Avila

Date:_____

Social Issues, World Issues, Governments, Churches

Current political /worldwide issues	Scripture References	What God Said

Intercessions Through Mary

"Most Immaculate heart of Mary, pray for us that we may grow closer to your Son, Jesus."

Date:_____

"Mary, please pray for."

Person or Issue	Specific Prayer Request

Daily Scriptures

"Be Still and Know that I am God." —Psalm 46:10

Date: _____

Scripture Passage: _____

Reflections

- *My heart:*

- *My head:*

- *My hand:*

Answer to Prayers

"Prayer unites us." —Pop Francis

Date:_____

Prayers that God has Answered:

Confessions

"Those who hope in the Lord will review their strength. They will soar on wings like eagles." —Isaiah 40:31

Date:_____

My Confession:

Thoughts on self-improvement:

Praise and Thanksgiving

"The best way to show gratitude to God and people is to accept everything with joy." —Mother Theresa

Date:_____

Today I am grateful for:

I will try to give thanks by:

Weekly Prayer Log

"To be a Christian without prayer is no more possible than to be alive without breathing." – Martin Luther

Week:_____

Day	Morning	Evening
Sunday		
Monday		
Tuesday		
Wednesday		
Thursday		
Friday		
Saturday		

Weekly Rosary Mysteries Chart

The Church sets aside Rosary Days to help in praying the Rosary. This is the chart for Ordinary Time

Day	Rosary Mystery	Complete?
Sunday	Glorious Mysteries	
Monday	Joyful Mysteries	
Tuesday	Sorrowful Mysteries	
Wednesday	Glorious Mysteries	
Thursday	Luminous Mysteries	
Friday	Sorrowful Mysteries	
Saturday	Joyful Mysteries	

Daily Prayer

"Prayer is an act of love." -Saint Teresa of Avila

Date:_____

Prayer for Other

Who is God Placing on my Heart?	Scripture References	What God Said

Daily Prayers

"Prayer is an act of love." -Saint Teresa of Avila

Date:_____

Prayer for Myself (Personal Issues and Needs)

What am I praying for?	Scripture References	What God Said

Daily Prayers

"Prayer is an act of love." -Saint Teresa of Avila

Date:_____

Social Issues, World Issues, Governments, Churches

Current political /worldwide issues	Scripture References	What God Said

Intercessions Through Mary

"Most Immaculate heart of Mary, pray for us that we may grow closer to your Son, Jesus."

Date:_____

"Mary, please pray for."

Person or Issue	Specific Prayer Request

Daily Scriptures

"Be Still and Know that I am God." —Psalm 46:10

Date: _____

Scripture Passage: _____

Reflections

- *My heart:*

- *My head:*

- *My hand:*

Answer to Prayers

"Prayer unites us." —Pop Francis

Date:_____

Prayers that God has Answered:

Confessions

"Those who hope in the Lord will review their strength. They will soar on wings like eagles." —Isaiah 40:31

Date:_____

My Confession:

Thoughts on self-improvement:

Praise and Thanksgiving

"The best way to show gratitude to God and people is to accept everything with joy." —Mother Theresa

Date: _____

Today I am grateful for:

I will try to give thanks by:

Made in the USA
Middletown, DE
01 January 2025